A Guide to the Eateries of Venice

Michela Scibilia

Venezia
Osterie & Dintorni
**A Guide to the Eateries
of Venice**

concept, graphic design and layout
Michela Scibilia

editors
Chiara Barbieri
Luisa Bellina
Andrea Montagnani

good photographs
Daniele Resini
Marc Smith

maps and other photographs
Michela Scibilia

english translation
Giles Watson

editorial consultant
Livio Scibilia

fonts and symbols
Scala Sans (Martin Majoor, 1993)
Keko (Paola Scibilia, 2002)

printed by
Grafiche Vianello
Treviso
ISBN 88-7200-123-4

advisors and companions at table
Elisabetta Ballarin
Chiara Barbieri
Luisa Bellina
Franco Bellino
Marie Brandolini
Monica Briata
Monica Cesari
Sara Cossiga
Franco Dalle Vacche
Jonathan Del Mar
Paola Fortuna
Elena Fumagalli
Vincenzo Giannotti
Luca Grinzato
Anna e Giorgio Ferrari
Giovanni Keller
Gudrun Kosmus
Alessandra Magistretti
Vittorio Marchiori
Marta Moretti
Claudio Nobbio
Renzo Paparone
Alberto Pazzaglia
Adriana Pellizzon
Nicoletta Possumato
Marco Saba
Silvia Sarpellon
Manuel Vecchina
Angela Torcasio
Neda and Alfredo Zambon

The eateries selected are offered as personal suggestions. This guide is not an official publication for the promotion of trade or tourism, nor is it supported by any kind of sponsorship. The publisher and author decline any liability, of whatever nature and for whatever reason, deriving from the information and data contained in the guide. It's best to get these things cleared up straight away.

Comments and suggestions from readers are very welcome. Please note that the editorial policy outlined above means that we cannot accept paid advertisements.

This guide went to press in June 2004

To the children who will be born in Venice.

Contents

Presentation

Almost ten years have passed since the first edition of this book – and it shows. This version features many editorial and other changes while the suggestions of friends and readers have also been incorporated. I, too, have changed. The guide's philosophy, however, remains the same. The book was written for friends from beyond the lagoon who ask me for tips on where and what to eat. Obviously, if I had actually been writing notes for a friend, I might have made a few more pointed comments (such as "have a drink and a nibble at the bar but, for heaven's sake, don't attempt to sit down – table prices are appalling!"). With a little care, you'll still be able to read between the lines, though. This little manual also aims to help all those Venetians who, like me, are the victims of foresti, or friends from the mainland. Non-Venetians, who tend to treat the city as a cross between Florence and Disneyland, are soon out of their depth and begging for help. Often, their local contact will have little time to spare so this guide might be one way of keeping guests out of trouble for a whie. Over the past few years, it has been satisfying to see just how many people have found the guide useful, if only for the phone numbers.

The eccentric local phone book can make it surprisingly difficult to locate the number you need. Of course, booking is always advisable, if you don't want to tramp halfway across the city to find your destination has no tables free. It was not my intention to promote the eateries featured here, although I am very happy to make a small contribution to the fame of such deserving establishments. I have simply selected the places that I know and use personally, where I have eaten on many occasions, and on which I have received comments from my team of informal advisers. Sometimes, they have reported behaviour or details that differ from my own experience. As a regular customer, I may have enjoyed slightly preferential treatment. But there is more to it. When you get to know an osteria, you know what to order and what to avoid. Intuition and experience tell you what dishes are less likely to be successful. There is a risk of misleading non-Venetian diners who do not possess this background information.

I have tried not to be influenced by the experience of a single visit. Nevertheless –
dear restaurateurs who are reading this – remember that your customer
"is there on one day only and wants to be looked after, listened to and spoiled".
The diner doesn't need to know that the cook called in sick this morning
and the waiter is having hysterics.

There are no stars, top ten lists or marks out of a hundred in this guide.
Instead, I have tried to bring out the personality of each locale. Every place
mentioned has something that makes it special. It might be superb cooking,
or tables outside with stunning views, or a particularly simpatico host,
whereas others may offer great sandwiches or wines.

Again for eatery owners, here are some bar snacks we hope will disappear:
"shrimp" made from crab sticks, baby carrots, improbable crab "claws", croquets,
Ascoli olives (fried straight from the freezer in elderly oil) and so on, particularly
if presented as "traditional Venetian cicheti". Apart from being uninspiring on the
palate, such fare lies heavy on the stomach.

Smart operators have long realised that an osteria can be very profitable.
We are seeing typical eateries opening now where once Chinese restaurants
flourished. These places consider themselves typical because they flaunt copper
kitchenware hanging from the ceiling and have a vaguely rustic atmosphere.
The "typical" cuisine usually comes out of the freezer, though.

Sadly, there are many such carbon-copy eateries, run by inscrutable managers
with "here today, gone tomorrow" waiters.
In contrast, the soul of a good osteria comes from people rather than the ambience
or the accoutrements.

It is the owner – and the owner's little quirks and eccentricities – that make
a place unique. The owner gets to know the regulars, adjusting the menu
and wines to suit them.

That is why this guide gives such prominence to photographs, often portraying
the locale's owner, or its equally distinctive clientele.
For the guide, I have deliberately selected a wide range of eateries.
Some serve only drinks; others offer full meals with all the trimmings.

Some are serious threats to the customer's solvency – but only the best have
been included and all offer a delightfully unforgettable dining experience –
whereas others are surprisingly inexpensive.

There has been a marked rise in the number of osterie that pay particular attention
to wines and spirits, cheeses, cold meats and territory-specific seasonal produce –
and even niche products – in response to growing consumer awareness.

We are now seeing fish carpaccio, schie, moeche, cave-matured cheeses, castraure,
botoli, carleti and sparasi – not always cheap but quality has its price –
accompanied by wine lists that were once undreamt-of. The leading actors in these
changes are the various associations that promote the culture of taste at all levels,
with Slow Food (www.slowfood.com) showing the way.

A satisfied diner will leave a modest or generous tip on the table to show
appreciation. But the restaurateur, too, can offer a discount, depending
on his or her appreciation of the diner.

The struggle to discourage too many tourists has prompted some owners to adopt
a debatable, but perhaps necessary, pricing policy that goes far beyond waiving
the service charge for Venetians, or offering a complimentary grappa.
The locals' discount can be as much as fifty per cent.

And so, aspiring diners, if you want to know where I like to go to eat or enjoy
a drink, slip this guide into your pocket. It is not, I repeat, either complete
or particularly objective. It is simply intended to be informative and useful.

My aim is to show that there are still places in Venice – actually, the number
is growing – where you can go to drink and eat, perhaps standing at the bar,
without risking your health or finances, despite a cost of living that is higher
than anywhere else in Italy.

I hope that your own personal experience will be as pleasant and, indeed,
memorable as my own. We are now going to set off on a journey of discovery
in a city behind whose tourist-dazzling façade lies a daily life of customs
and habits well worth protecting and recovering.

Michela Scibilia

Frequently asked questions

or tasty snippets to get you started

Where can I find a really traditional osteria?

da Dante and da Lele

Where can I get a serious glass of wine?

All'Aciugheta, Al Bancogiro, Cavatappi, Alla Mascareta, Al Prosecco
and La Rivista

Which restaurants have the best-stocked cellars?

Top of the list are the Fiaschetteria Toscana and Da Fiore. Then come Agli
Alboretti, La Colombina, Al Covo, Corte Sconta, San Marco, Santa Marina,
Vini da Gigio, Alle Testiere and Vino Vino

*Which establishments are more or less unchanged since
the first edition of the guide?*

Only thirty-four out of one hundred and thirty featured. All'Aciugheta, Antiche
Carampane, All'Arco, Assassini, Algiubagiò, Bacaretto, Al Bentigodi, Da Bes,
Birreria Forst, Alla Botte, Corte Sconta, Al Covo, Da Dante, The Fiddler's
Elbow, Fiore, Da Fiore, Fontana, Harry's Bar, L'Incontro, Alla Madonna,
Al Nono Risorto, Olandese Volante, Paradiso Perduto, Alla Patatina, Da Pinto,
Gislon, Ai Rusteghi, San Basilio, Alle Testiere, Ca' d'Oro, Vini da Arturo, Vini
da Gigio, Vino Vino and Alla Zucca

Which places have opened recently or are under new management?

Angiò, L'Angolo di Tanit, La Bitta, Boccadoro, Cavatappi, La Colombina,
Ae Do Marie, Al Fontego dei Pescaori, Mirai, Il Refolo, Rioba and San Marco

What about non-Italian cooking?
Mirai (Japanese), Los Murales (Mexican), Sahara (Syrian),
Frary's Bar (middle eastern)

Where can we meet for an aperitif?

exclusive	Harry's Bar (for a Bellini),
	Monaco – Gran Canal (sip a Martini to live piano music)
traditional	All'Aciugheta, Da Alberto, All'Arco, Alla Botte, Cantinone,
	Do Mori, Alla Mascareta, Vitae, Ca' d'Oro, Al Volto
	or Cavatappi
alternative	Da Lele

Dove xe che magna i mureri? ("Where do builders go to eat?", in other words,
"Where can I find good, plain cooking that attracts building workers?" In practice,
these eateries are also patronised by office workers and students)
Mistrà and Ae Do Marie

And what about a pizza with the old class from school?
Casin dei Nobili, La Perla and Al Nono Risorto

Where do we go if we fancy a pizza in a scenic spot that will make
us really feel on holiday?
Acqua Pazza or Il Refolo

What about a traditional fish meal in a proper restaurant
with a white tablecloth and all the trimmings?
Alla Madonna or Da Remigio

Where do you suggest for Sunday lunch?

Acqua Pazza, Agli Alboretti, Anice Stellato, Da Bepi, Le Bistrot de Venise, Boccadoro, Casin dei Nobili, La Colombina, Al Covo, La Cusina, Al Diporto, Fiaschetteria Toscana, Al Fontego dei Pescaori, Frary's Bar, Harry's Bar and Harry's Dolci, Da Ignazio, L'Incontro, Alla Madonna, 'E Masaniello, Mirai, Mistrà, Monaco–Gran Canal, Los Murales, Al Nono Risorto, Oliva Nera, Al Paradiso Perduto, Quadri, Il Refolo, Da Remigio, Ribò, Rioba, Rivetta, La Rivista, Sahara, Dai Tosi , Vini da Gigio or Vino Vino

What are the favourite hangouts of Venice's movers and shakers?

Antiche Carampane, Da Fiore, Harry's Bar, Vini da Arturo and Vini da Gigio

... and where do the local gourmets eat?

Agli Alboreti, Al Covo, Fiaschetteria Toscana, Da Fiore, Santa Marina and Alle Testiere

... where can I grab a quick lunch in the city (ie, in the San Marco area)?

Assassini, A la Campana, Da Carla, Vino Vino or Vitae

Can you suggest somewhere intimate for dinner à deux?

Alle Testiere or Monaco-Gran Canal

Which restaurants can you get to in a boat (a gondola, of course)?

Anice Stellato, Da Baffo, Al Bancogiro, Canottieri, Cantinone – già Schiavi, Da Còdroma, Fontana, Al Fontego dei Pescaori, Frary's Bar, Da Lele, Dalla Marisa, Al Paradiso Perduto, Ai Postali, Il Refolo, Ribò, Rioba, Rivetta, Sahara, Suziecafè, Vini da Gigio and Alla Zucca

Which restaurants can you get to in a motorboat (slowly)?
Algiubagiò, Angiò, Al Chioschetto, Harry's Dolci, Mistrà, Los Murales
and San Basilio

Where can I listen to live music?
Al Paradiso Perduto, Ruga Rialto and Suziecafè

Where can a large group feel at home?
Alla Madonna, Al Paradiso Perduto, Ruga Rialto, Corte Sconta or Los Murales

Where can we get something to eat after eleven at night?
Le Bistrot de Venise, La Colombina, Il Refolo or Sahara

... and is there anywhere to get a drink after midnight?
Da Baffo, Le Bistrot de Venise, Al Chioschetto, La Colombina,
Ai Do Draghi, Alla Mascareta, Olandese Volante, Al Paradiso Perduto,
Il Refolo or Vitae

Where can we go for a decent beer?
Birreria Forst, The Fiddler's Elbow or Olandese Volante

Is there anywhere that caters for those with a sweet tooth?
Al Bacareto, Bentigodi, Fiaschetteria Toscana, Da Fiore, Harry's Dolci,
Monaco-Gran Canal, Vini da Arturo or Alla Zucca

Where can we sit outside with plenty of space to enjoy a drink in the open air?
Al Chioschetto, Angiò, Al Bancogiro, Da Baffo, La Cantina, Ai Do Draghi, Elio,
The Fiddler's Elbow, Harry's Dolci, Olandese Volante, Postali, Prosecco,
Rivista and Suziecafè

... and for an al fresco *meal?*

Acqua Pazza, Boccadoro, Canottieri, La Cusina, Al Diporto, Fontana, Harry's Dolci, L'Incontro, Ignazio, Marisa, 'E Masaniello, Los Murales, Al Paradiso Perduto, Il Refolo, Rioba, La Rivista or Sahara

Where can you eat well without breaking the bank?
Good question

How do we go about making a giro di ombre *(a tour of local* osterie)?
It doesn't require much organisation. Start early, at about half past six: almost all the osterie close before nine in the evening and the ones that offer restaurant facilities suspend bar service. Then just follow your nose round the bars, and have an *ombra* and a *cichetto* at each stop...

San Marco: Al Bacareto – Fiore – Vino Vino – Assassini – Al Volto – Vitae – A la Campana – Cavatappi – Alla Botte – Ai Rusteghi

San Polo: Al Bancogiro – Da Pinto – Elio – Do Mori – All'Arco – Ruga Rialto – Vivaldi – Alla Patatina

Dorsoduro: Al Pantalon – Ai Do Draghi – La Bitta – Ai Vini Padovani – Cantinone – Al Chioschetto

Castello: All'Aciugheta – Alla Mascareta – Al Portego

Cannaregio: Al Ponte – Da Alberto – Ca' d'Oro – La Cantina – Al Paradiso Perduto – Anice Stellato – Bentigodi

The eateries of Venice ...

legend

🖐 excellent value for money.

[€35] 🍴 trattoria/restaurant or similar establishment where you can eat a full meal at table in a dignified manner. Only eateries in this category have the average cost (in €) of a meal, including antipasto, primo, secondo, side dish, sweet, table charge and service, but excluding wine and other drinks.
In some cases, the symbol has not been awarded, even though the locale could have been included in the category. In these cases, our suggestion is to eat at the bar, rather than at table.
A similar system has been applied to the osteria-style establishments.
The prices quoted may look excessive but it should be remembered that customers will usually order only one or two dishes.
Restaurant opening hours are given only when the restaurant also offers bar facilities. The eatery will then be open outside the 12.30 pm–2.30 pm and 7.30 pm–10.30 pm mealtimes (bar service is normally suspended when meals are being served).

🍷 It is possible to have just a drink at the bar.

🍾 Interesting wine list.

☼ Tables indoors and *al fresco*.

℺ Children welcome. The ambience, service and menu offered ensure adults and smaller guests can co-exist. As a rule, it is advisable to eat out with children at midday.

NEW Recently opened (or recent change of management).
The guide includes some eateries that have made a promising start and whose enthusiasm deserves encouragement. As these locales may be subject to adjustments or changes, we have indicated them with a special symbol.

♡ An *osteria* of which the author is particularly fond. This symbol is not an indication of quality, as all the locales in the guide have been selected for (nearly) objective reasons. These are simply the author's personal favourites.

all'Aciugheta 🍷🍴

+39 041 5224292, Castello 4357, Campo Santi Filippo e Giacomo
⏰ 8 am–12 pm, open all week

The pizzeria All'Aciugheta feeds a fair proportion of the noisy multilingual hordes that fill the streets and alleys behind San Marco. Think local, act like those who know the ropes and, ignoring the tablefuls of tourists indoors and outside, head straight for the bar. Select one of the excellent wines from the dozen or so Gianni has brought up from his cellar and sip it appreciatively, perhaps with a meatball, a delicious *crostino* or one of the bar's great cheeses.

Of course, if the mini *aciugheta* pizzas have just arrived, you might want to try one.

Acqua Pazza [€ 68] 🍴🍷☀

+39 041 2770688, San Marco 3808, Campo Sant'Angelo ⏰ 12 am–15 pm and 19 pm–23pm, closed Monday

Antonio has brought all the *simpatia* of Naples to his two restaurants (he also runs 'E Masaniello at Santo Stefano). His pizza, made exclusively with fresh tomato and buffalo mozzarella, is seriously good (€ 11–14), but his other offerings are equally exciting: baked mussels in pepper, salmon with onions and capers, fried vegetables in batter (yummy), bucatini pasta with scorpionfish, linguine with lobster, stuffed squid and grilled or steamed *mazzancolle* prawns. To crown it all, you can enjoy your meal under snow-white awnings in one of Venice's brightest and most central *campi*.

da Alberto [€ 32] 🍴🍷

+39 041 5238153, Cannaregio 5401,
Calle Larga Giacinto Gallina ● 10 am–3 pm
and 6 pm–11 pm, closed Sunday

Located between Campo Santi
Giovanni e Paolo and the
beautiful Miracoli church, this
trattoria provides comfort and
refreshment for customers from
Venice and elsewhere. The bar is
well stocked with fried sardines
and *baccalà*, excellent meatballs,
shrimp and boiled *latti di seppia*.
You will find *nerveti* with onion or
museto in winter, and *castraure* in

spring. If you decide to take a table, there is a range of
pastas and risottos, with fish or shellfish and vegetables,
mixed seafood fries, grilled fish, steamed cuttlefish and
baccalà with *polenta*.

agli Alboretti [€ 55] 🍴🥂☀

+39 041 5230058 – 5210158, Dorsoduro 882, Rio Terà Antonio Foscarini,
closed Wednesday and Thursday morning

This restaurant near the Accademia was once the haunt
of artists. Today, the retro elegance, impeccable service
and enviable kitchen attract a clientele that knows its

food. The quality and freshness of the raw materials are a given. Special attention is devoted to
balancing textures and flavours, further enhancing them with sauces and spices. Try the *baccalà
mantecato* with a timbale of crispy potatoes on a bed of stewed *radicchio trevigiano*, pumpkin risotto
with diamonds of tarragon-flavoured cuttlefish, or baked sea bream with spiced bread and brandy
baked mussels. The cheese trolley will satisfy even the most discriminating. Finally, the wine list is a
connoisseur's delight, with particular attention
lavished on *vini da meditazione* and grappas.

Algiubagiò ♟ ☼ ⚲

+39 041 5236084, Cannaregio 5039, Fondamente Nuove,
🕐 6.30 am–11 pm, open all week

On a clear day in late winter, it is relaxing to linger on the Fondamente Nuove, on the broad wood terrace of the Algiubagiò, and reflect on life as you gaze on the northern lagoon and distant mountains. Here by the *vaporetto* landing, commuting workers jostle with tourists as they leave for, or arrive from, the islands of Murano, Burano, Torcello and Sant'Erasmo. Eat at the bar, which offers large and small *panini*, as well as *tramezzini*, a few hot dishes, uncomplicated salads, ice creams, draught beer and – for tobacco addicts who contrive to run out on a Sunday – cigarettes.

Angiò ♟ ◗ ☼

+39 041 2778555, Castello 2142, Ponte della Veneta Marina
🕐 7 am–9 pm (in summer, until 12 pm), closed Tuesday

Brother and sister team Andrea and Giovanna run the only decent eatery on this long, ultra-touristy stretch of lagoon front running from San Marco to the Arsenale. Angiò offers a great view to go with your aperitif, *panini*, salad or Irish beer. Good selection of wines, cheeses and cold meats.

all'Angolo ♟ ☼

+39 041 5220710, San Marco 3464, Campo Santo Stefano
🕐 6.30 am–9 pm (in summer, until 10 pm), closed Saturday

A favourite meeting place, not just for its strategic position but also for the friendly atmosphere that sets it apart from more pretentious neighbours. The *spritz* is legendary.
Panini, mini pizzas, *tramezzini* and a glass of beer accompany your people-watching.

l'Angolo di Tanit [€ 44]

+39 041 720504, Cannaregio 1885, Calle dell'Aseo,
Closed Tuesday and Sunday

At last, we can sample genuine Sicilian food
here in Venice. The friendly restaurant-cum-
osteria recently opened by Battista – who is,
of course, from Sicily – in a quiet *calle* just off
the Strada Nuova offers a limited menu that
changes every day. You might find caponata,
(eggplants, celery, tomatoes, onions, capers
and olives, sautéed in oil and served in a
sweet and sour dressing), spaghetti with
pesto trapanese (made with fresh tomatoes,
garlic, basil, almonds and olive oil), a fish couscous, tuna
with capers and olives and, to round off the meal, *cannoli*.
Friendly atmosphere and a small range of Sicilian wines.

Anice Stellato [€ 34]

+39 041 720744, Cannaregio 3272, Fondamenta della Sensa
● 10 am–2 pm and 7 pm–10 pm, closed Monday and Tuesday

The name – it means "star-anise" – says it all. Spices and aromatic herbs perfume your *carpaccio*
of tuna or swordfish, fresh salmon, the sea bream and steamed *barboni*, tagliatelle with scampi
and courgette flowers or fish risotto. Creative cuisine and care over raw materials and preparation

have in a few short years turned this small,
out-of-the-way restaurant on the attractive
Fondamenta della Sensa into a successful
enterprise. Run by a well-organised family
team, the Anice Stellato is also noted for
giving value for money. So it is essential
to book well in advance. Between meals,
the bar is always open for *ombre* and
cicheti. A great place to eat.

Antiche Carampane [€ 47] 🍴☀♡

+39 041 5240165, San Polo 1911, Rio Terà
de le Carampane, closed Sunday and Monday

Let yourself be drawn into the maze of
long, narrow *calli*, dark *sotoporteghi*, courtyards and *rio terà* that protect the city's former red-light district. If you have managed to follow the directions, you will end up at this oasis of welcoming calm. Awaiting you are elegant ambience and the very freshest of fish, cooked with a master's touch. Monkfish al *cartoccio* in a crust of parmesan cheese, wonderfully delicate mixed fried fish and fresh spring vegetables are some of the delights on the menu.

all'Arco 🍷☀♡

+39 041 5205666, San Polo 436, Calle dell'Occhialer
○ 8 am–3.30 pm, closed Sunday

A pocket handkerchief-sized *osteria* near Rialto. The few tables in the *calle* are always busy during business hours at the market and in the early evening. Francesco Pinto is an experienced landlord who keeps very drinkable unbottled wines. Above all, his *cicheti* are some of the best around. Choose from *panini*, hot *crostini* with robiola cheese, mushrooms and truffle-aromatised olive oil, *mozzarella in carrozza*, or envelopes of asparagus and courgette flowers filled with ricotta cheese and smoked speck ham. Connoisseurs will also find ultra-traditional *cicheti* of *spiensa*, *tetina* and *rumegal*.

Arte della Pizza 🍷

+39 041 5246520, Cannaregio 1896,
○ 11 am–2 pm and 5 pm–9 pm, closed Monday

Excellent snacking pizza sold by the slice. The pizzas are fresh out of the oven. Toppings range from the traditional to the adventurous, such as *radicchio di Treviso* and grana cheese, or potato and rosemary without tomato. Take-away pizzas are available for spur-of-the-moment parties.

Assassini [€ 40] 🍴 🍷 🧴 ☀

+39 041 5287986, San Marco 3695,
Rio Terà dei Assassini, ⏺ 11.30 am–3 pm
and 6.45 pm–11.30 pm, closed Sunday
and Saturday morning

An *osteria* with more atmosphere
than imagination. Monday's
menu features soup and white
meat. Tuesday is braised beef.
On Wednesday, there's *pasta
e fasioi*, *nerveti* and *museto*.
Thursday is boiled beef or
baccalà. On Friday and Saturday,
it's fish. Limited selection of
wines and cheeses.

al Bacareto [€ 48] 🍴 🍷 ☀

+39 041 5289336, San Marco 3447, Calle de le Boteghe ⏺ 7.30 am–11 pm, closed Saturday evening and Sunday

For over a century, this historic *bacaro* has been refreshing – morning, noon and night –
local customers and the hordes of tourists who pass through Campo Santo Stefano or visit the
exhibitions at the nearby Palazzo Grassi. At the bar, enjoy an *ombra* of unbottled Veneto or Friulian
wine and classic *cicheti*. You are sure to find rice, potato, meat and spinach balls, battered and fried
baccalà and other fish-based snacks. The fried sardines are universally acknowledged as the best
in town. Tradition is the keynote at the tables, too, with *bigoli in salsa*, cuttlefish cooked in its ink
with *polenta*, Venetian-style liver and other delights.
Service is informal and extremely courteous.

da Baffo ♟ ☼

+39 041 5208862, San Polo 2346, Campo Sant'Agostin
◐ 7.30 am–2 am, closed Sunday

A noisy, smoke-filled beer and sandwich bar much beloved of students, upwardly mobile professionals and the occasional university lecturer. The morning's cappuccino-and-croissant customers are followed by office workers in search of a satisfying lunchtime *panino*. Life goes on and by early evening, people are sipping *spritz* or Belgian beer, which can be enjoyed until the wee small hours, either indoors or at a table in the *campo*. Winter evenings are enlivened by live jazz, rhythm and blues and fusion music.

al Bancogiro ⏢ ♟ ⓘ ☼

+39 041 5232061, San Polo 122, Campo San Giacometto ◐ 10.30 am–3 pm and 6.30 pm–12 pm, closed Sunday evening and Monday

This wine shop with kitchen beneath the porticos of the sixteenth-century Fabbriche Vecchie has two entrances. One is from the market and the church of San Giacometto; the other, with outside tables, faces the Canal Grande. Al Bancogiro stands on the site of one of Venice's, and perhaps history's, earliest trading banks and has kept the original name. Sip a glass of good wine at the bar, choosing from the bottles Andrea selects each day, or sit in the small, smoke-free dining room upstairs.

With a little patience (dishes – from € 11 to € 14 – are cooked to order), you will be enjoying delights prepared with ingredients fresh from the nearby fish and vegetable market: prawns with *castraure*, *carpaccio* of bass garnished with mixed aromatic herbs, *sarde incinte* ("pregnant" sardines stuffed with raisins, pine nuts, garlic, parsley and orange juice), creamed dentex, steamed fish salads or smoked American beef. There's also a limited range of cold meats and cheeses.

Bandierette [€ 28] 🍴 ☀

+39 041 5220619, Castello 6671,
Barbaria de le Tole ● closed Munday evening
and Tuesday

This is a typical neighbourhood
trattoria near Santi Giovanni
e Paolo. Plain and downright
anonymous on the outside, it is a
firm favourite with local residents.
There are other good reasons
for eating here, including the
affordable prices and the genuine
homestyle cooking – with an
added touch of imagination. The fish-based menu is uncomplicated,
with baked fan shell scallops, fried sardines, monkfish or grilled bass.
The tasty pastas include tagliatelle with scampi and spinach,
spaghetti with *canoce* or prawns and asparagus.

Bentigodi [€ 33] 🍴 🍷 ☀ ♀

041 716269, Cannaregio 1423, Calleselle ● 10.30 am–3 pm and 6 pm–12 pm, closed Sunday evening and Monday

Between the busy Rio Terà San Leonardo and the Ghetto lies one of the friendliest *osterie* in the
sestiere of Cannaregio. There are tables in the *calle* and two rooms inside, as well as a huge bar laden
with tempting *cicheti*. Your host, Elena, hails from Friuli and enjoys making soups and pasta sauces
from original combinations of ingredients. You might find swordfish and eggplant, baby squid
and *radicchio*, fan shell scallops and artichokes or scampi with courgette flowers in saffron.
The seasonal vegetables are many and various, as are the sweets.
Don't restrict yourself to the house wine when ordering the drinks.

da Bepi – Già 54 [€ 39] 🍴 ☀

+39 041 5285031, Cannaregio 4550, Campo Santi Apostoli, closed Thursday

Strategically positioned at Santi Apostoli, where three major routes intersect: one from Strada Nuova and the station, one from Rialto and one from Fondamente Nuove. This is a favoured spot where Venetians to sit at the outside tables and spot passersby while chatting with the young *oste*. The menu offers classic Venetian fish dishes, such as *canoce*, *caparossoli*, seafood risotto and cuttlefish with *polenta* but there are also concessions to simpler tastes, with *pasta e fasioi*, *gnocchi* with tomato or grilled steak also featured.

da Bes – Tre Spiedi [€ 35] 🍴

+39 041 5208035, Cannaregio 5906, Salizada San Cancian, closed Sunday evening and Monday

An old-fashioned trattoria run by two brothers who are married to two sisters. This friendly, unpretentious family team attracts a clientele of local habitués and particularly well-informed *foresti*. Mixed fish starters, such as *latti di seppia* and *folpeti*, the traditional *saor*, spaghetti with *caparossoli*, fish risottos and, of course, *baccalà*, are all on the menu. To round things off, have a *sgropìn*. Bookings not accepted.

Birreria Forst 🍷

+39 041 5230557, Castello 4540, Calle delle Rasse ● 10 am–11 pm, closed Saturday (only in winter and during August)

A welcome refuge in one of Venice's most tourist-infested *calli*, a stone's throw from Palazzo Ducale.
The black bread *tramezzini* with beef, roast pork or frankfurters and mustard are legendary, as are the French-style rolls and ambrogini – small, sweet rolls – with genuine, Consortium-branded *prosciutto crudo* from Parma and the four kinds of draught beer. Where better to grab a snack? If you want a coffee, though, you've come to the wrong place.

le Bistrot de Venise [€ 70]

+39 041 5236651, San Marco 4685, Calle dei Fabbri ● 10 am–1 am, open all week

Sergio has become increasingly enamoured of "antique" cooking, such as *pastelo de ostreghe* (oysters in batter), *tortin de risi* (rice cake) and *ambroyno* (chicken stuffed with plums, spices, dates and almonds). Luckily, his kitchen staff insist he should also offer a less ambitious menu of traditional dishes, catering for a wider market.

This is one of the few restaurants in Venice that can guarantee food cooked to order late at night – the doors close at half past midnight. Sergio arranges a wide range of cultural events, including book presentations, exhibitions of art and photography, poetry evenings and live music. Ask for the programme.

la Bitta [€ 40]

+39 041 5230531, Dorsoduro 2753a, Calle Lunga San Barnaba
● 6 pm–2 am, closed Sunday

An *osteria*-cum-restaurant with a limited menu of vegetable and meat dishes. You might find artichoke and grana cheese salad, penne pasta with smoked speck ham and pumpkin, or Irish fillet steak. The wine list is interesting and there are tasty *cicheti* at the bar.

27 –

Boccadoro [€ 50]

+39 041 5211021, Cannaregio 5405a, Campiello Widman, or dei Biri, closed Monday

This bright, new restaurant is in the broad *campo* on the way from the Miracoli church to the Fondamente Nuove ferry for the islands of the northern lagoon.

Chef Davide may be young but he is very professional. His menu puts the accent on the very freshest of fish. Actually, it is a shame to cook it so try his oysters, shrimp, fan shell scallops and raw swordfish or tuna. Or sample the grilled *canestrei*, *gnocchetti* with mussels or dory with *castraure*.

The prominence of Sardinian wines and cheeses in the range offered tells you where one of the partners hails from.

alla Botte [€ 35] 🍴🍷🍺

+39 041 5209775, San Marco 5482,
Calle della Bissa ● 10 am–3 pm
and 5 pm–11 pm, closed Sunday evening
and Thursday

It's not hard to find this *osteria* of an evening. Just follow the young people heading here from Campo San Bartolomio. The bar is always full, especially from early evening until closing time. Elbow your way through to the meatballs, *bovoleti*, potatoes and *folpeti*. Alternatively, go to the small dining area for a plate of tagliatelle with scallops or scampi and cherry tomatoes, *sepe nere*, or tripe in parmesan cheese.

Ca' d'Oro – alla Vedova [€ 32] 🍴🍷♡

+39 041 5285324, Cannaregio 3912, Ramo Ca' d'Oro ● 11.30 am–2.30 pm and 6.30 pm–10.30 pm, closed Thursday
and Sunday morning

The best-known of Cannaregio's historic *osterie* and a mandatory stop on any *giro di ombre* in Strada Nuova. *Foresti* like the warm, characteristic ambience and the wide range of *cicheti*, which covers almost the entire gamut of traditional Venetian gastronomy. There is whitebait, meatballs, *folpeti consi*, grilled, boiled and stuffed vegetables, *castraure* and artichoke bottoms (in season), *sarde in saor*, *baccalà*, skewered shrimp, *sepe roste* (grilled cuttlefish) and more. Not to mention the many unbottled wines. If you want more than a snack at the bar, you are well advised to book a table in advance.

a la Campana [€ 22/40] 🍴🍷

+39 041 5285170, San Marco 4720,
Calle dei Fabbri ● closed Sunday

A classic *osteria*, from the dark
wood-panelled walls to the paper
napkins, with young, active owners.
The traditional menu includes
tagliolini pasta with fan shell
scallops and scampi, steamed tripe
and *baccalà*. The midday menu is
less expensive, offering quick
meals for workers from the area's
many offices. In the evening, there
is pasta cooked to order, fresh fish and a little more peace.

la Cantina 🍷🍴☀♡

+39 041 5228258, Cannaregio 3689, Campo San Felice ● 10 am–10 pm, closed Sunday

A wonderful spot to sit at one of the tables outside and smile at passersby hurrying along the
Strada Nuova as you sip a glass of Prosecco, a mug of draught beer, or perhaps a bottle suggested
by Andrea. Savour one of the mouthwatering small *panini*, or a *bruschetta* with roast pork, smoked
beef, gorgonzola, anchovies, baby artichokes, olive pâté, sun-dried tomatoes, or with quail's eggs
and grilled asparagus, burrata cheese and *aringa sciocca* (unsalted herring), pears with parmesan
cheese and horseradish *mostarda*. If you are lucky, you might find fresh *tartufi di mare*
(*Venus verrucosa* shellfish), collected
by hand.

Regulars like to perch on the stools at
the bar, swapping chit-chat with
Francesco and watching him at work
as he prepares his irresistible *crostini*.

Mauro Lorenzon

>> The irrepressible, Jesolo-born Mauro Lorenzon is the creator of Enoiteche, an association of wine shops committed to serving a roster of twenty-four types of wines by the – appropriately shaped – glass.

Mauro can now be found at the Mascareta >> see p. 42

Canottieri [€ 20/40] 🍴 🍷 ☼

+39 041 717999, Cannaregio 690, Fondamenta del Macello
● 8 am–3 pm and 7 pm–11 pm, closed Monday evening and Sunday

This used to be a quiet bar – Venice sinks into the lagoon a few metres further on. Since the area was colonised by the university, though, the morning air has echoed to orders for croissants, *panini*, and salads (€ 5) from book-toting clients. The Venetian-style evening menu is more expensive. Spacious, comfortable interior with long wooden tables, as well as the ones that look onto the *fondamenta*.

Cantinone – già Schiavi 🍷 🍾

+39 041 5230034, Dorsoduro 992, Ponte San Trovaso ● 8.30 am–8.30 pm, closed Sunday afternoon

Is there still anyone who hasn't heard of the Cantinone? The walls are hidden behind shelves

of bottles, providing drinkers with an opportunity to pass the time in appreciative contemplation. The range is astounding, embracing everyday wines and bottles for special occasions. It's hard to leave without at least a bottle of Prosecco di Valdobbiadene in your bag. Ten or so wines are available by the glass, to wash down your *tocheto* of mortadella, or cheese, or the *crostini* with *baccalà* in various guises.

– 30

da Carla [€ 25] 🍴🍷🍸

+39 041 5237855, San Marco 1535, Corte Contarina
● 8 am–10.30 pm, closed Sunday

Da Carla is just round the corner from Piazza San Marco
but, perhaps because it is hidden by a small *sotoportego*,
the customers are almost all locals. They come for a quick,
tasty meal of cold pasta or lasagne, or the excellent
tramezzini and *panini*. There ten or so good wines
to choose from and *cicheti* are always on hand.

Casin dei Nobili [€ 36] 🍴🍷☀

+39 041 2411841, Dorsoduro 2765, Sotoportego del Casin dei Nobili
● 12 am–11.30 pm, closed Monday

Just beyond the *sotoportego* that leads from Campo
San Barnaba to Calle de la Toletta, this capacious
osteria with its own garden looks onto the bridge
and canal. Much beloved of students who frequent
Campo Santa Margherita for its friendly atmosphere
and good pizzas (€ 4.50–8, available evenings only
during the week, and midday and evenings from
Friday to Sunday), Casin dei Nobili also offers
a few other options.

Cavatappi 🍷🍸☀ 🏮

041 2960252, San Marco 525, campo della Guerra ● 9 am–12 pm, closed Sunday evening and Monday

Marco and Francesca opened this modern, well-lit bar-cum-*enoteca* (with kitchen) a while ago.
Their enthusiasm is undeniable: they even organise tastings.
The bar caters for snack attacks with excellently made small *panini* and *tramezzini*. Locals gather
here in the evening for an aperitif or an after-dinner drink. At midday, the tables are filled with the
neighbourhood's shopkeepers, who appreciate the brief menu of rice and pasta-based dishes (€ 7)
– on Thursday, the pasta is freshly made – and the light but tasty main courses (€ 10), chicken
salad, stuffed squid, generous salads (€ 8) and desserts made on the premises. Every two months,
thirty wines are available for tasting, with cheeses and cold meats from a different region of Italy.

al Chioschetto ♟ ☀

Dorsoduro 1406, Fondamenta Zattere
● 7.30 am–1 am

Since various university departments moved to the area, this small kiosk on the canalside and its extensive deck have been swamped by students sunning themselves between lectures, or enjoying the cool Zattere evenings while munching on *panini*, *piadine* and toasted sandwiches.

But it is also a favourite spot for lone strollers in search of an appropriate setting for their silent musings. Convince yourself by pausing here for an aperitif and gazing over the Giudecca canal, from Marghera to the island of San Giorgio.

da Còdroma ♟

+39 041 5246789, Dorsoduro 2540, Ponte del Soccorso
● 8 am–12 pm, closed Sunday

Bruschette, *panini* and *mozzarella in carrozza*. But if you're feeling in need of comfort on a cold winter's morning, a cup of hot chocolate will raise your spirits. You'll usually find noisy groups of students here so stay away on graduation days. Practical jokes are traditional.

– 32

la Colombina [€ 57] 🍴 🍸 ☀

+39 041 2750622, Cannaregio 1828, Corte del Pegoloto ● 7 pm–2 am, open all week

Bruno and his son Giorgio have been running this tastefully decorated restaurant and *enoteca* for some time. It faces onto a small, cool courtyard, well away from the bustle of Strada Nuova. There's an interesting wine list to match with the range of cheeses and fruit compotes, *bruschette* and *crostini* (with a Tuscan touch that tells you where the owners come from) or hot and cold dishes. These vary, depending on the meat and fish on offer in the local market, but the signature dish is the mythical *fiorentina* of Chianina beef, from Tozzetti, the Mercatale Val di Pesa butcher. And all this is at your disposal until two in the morning.

Corte Sconta [€ 52] 🍴🍷☀♡

+39 041 5227024, Castello 3886, Calle del Pestrin, closed Sunday and Monday

A cult *osteria*, partly for its position and partly for the name, which is also
emblematic of the many *sconto* (hidden) corners of the Venetian cityscape.
The friendly owners serve up expertly made versions of the lagoon's
traditional cuisine. The list of starters is endless, with marinated anchovies, *granseola* pâté,
schie with *polenta*, *latti di seppia*, *garusoli*, *sarde in saor*, *canoce* and more. You can try them all
and have a "tasting meal". *Primi* include gnocchetti with baby squid, tagliolini (all fresh pasta
is made on the premises) with scallops and artichokes, and *bigoli in salsa* while the *secondi* are
equally impressive. Grilled or fried fish is flanked by herb-baked baby red mullet and dory in sweet
and sour sauce. Finish with a traditional *zabaion* and kosher biscuits.
There are 110 wines on the list and a fine selection of grappas.

al Covo [€ 75] 🍴🍷☀

+39 041 5223812, Castello 3968, Campiello della Pescaria, closed Wednesday and Thursday

A small restaurant in Campiello della Pescheria behind Riva degli Schiavoni, Al Covo is a magnet
for gourmets from Venice and beyond. The menu is based on fish – never farmed – in traditional,
and often neglected, dishes that have been skilfully re-interpreted to bring out the freshness and
fragrance of the raw material. The fish and shellfish crudités with
vegetables, the fish soups, the *gnocchi* with fillets of *gò*, the steamed
eel, the fried and the grilled fish are all superb.

The desserts are outstanding and "sublime" is the only word
for the chocolate cake with dark chocolate sauce.

There are 300 wines, forty spirits and ten olive oils to choose from.

A word of warning – Al Covo does not accept credit cards.

la Cusina [€ 113] 🍴 ☀

+39 041 2400759, San Marco 2200, Calle del Traghetto, open all week

The restaurant of the Hotel Europa e Regina, La Cusina is striving to acquire a personality of its own. You have to go down a small *calle*, or through the hotel, to find it so this tends to be a quiet, sheltered spot. Once inside, you will have one of the city's finest dining views, looking across the surface of the lagoon to the church of the Salute.

Sit back and drink in the panorama. The menu is tempting and sophisticated, the portions generous, so tuck into your Scotch salmon with candied cherry tomatoes and lobster, cream of peas with prawns and cress, loin of lamb fragranced with oranges and paprika and accompanied with glazed spring onions, fried scampi and squid with eggplant and fried sage, or green tea mousse with apple sauce. The brief but interesting low-calorie menu is also worth a glance. But if you are looking for something a little less daunting, you can take a seat on the terrace of the adjoining hotel and order something from the bar menu (€ 14–30).

What about a chicken salad, a shrimp cocktail, a grilled fillet steak or a roastbeef sandwich? Expertly made cocktails are also on hand.

da Dante 🍷 ☀

+39 041 5285163, Castello 2877, Corte Nova ● 8 am–9 pm, closed Sunday

Da Dante is one of the few *osterie* to have kept its authentic, working-class character. Tucked away in a court in San Lorenzo, at Castello, it lies beyond a *sotoportego* with an altar to a *madonna nera*, or Black Virgin. Ask for a glass of white or red and a *meso ovo*, an *aciugheta*, a cuttlefish, a plate of *bovoleti*, or *nerveti*, or perhaps *garùsoli*. Then watch the old-timers playing cards and listen to their murmured comments on the never-ending comedy of life in Venice.

al Diporto [€ 38] 🍴☀

+39 041 5285978, Sant'Elena, Calle Cengio 25–27, ● 10.30 am–3 pm and
6.30 pm–12 pm, closed Monday

You're with a group of friends in the Biennale gardens,
and you're looking for something to eat and a cool white
wine to wash it down with. Look no further. Al Diporto is
an unpretentious trattoria, always crowded after
matches at the nearby stadium and on warm summer's
evenings. Try a mixed seafood *antipasto* (*canoce*, *folpeti*
and shrimp), fried fish and a salad.

ai Do Draghi 🍷☀

+39 041 5289731, Dorsoduro 3665, Campo Santa Margherita
● 7.30 am–10 pm (until 2 am in summer), closed Thursday (only in winter)

There's something of the Parisian bistrot about Ai Do Draghi, perhaps
because the customers are bespectacled, book-laden types. Misunderstood
academics or students late for lectures? Sip a draught beer, or one of the forty
wines by the glass, and munch a *tramezzino* with smoked speck ham, brie
and rocket, or fresh vegetables and buffalo mozzarella, as you discuss your
conclusions with a friend in the bar or outside on Campo Santa Margherita.

Do Mori 🍷🍴

+39 041 5225401, San Polo 429, Calle dei Do Mori
● 8.30 am–8.30 pm, closed Sunday

Venetians will tell you, "it isn't the *osteria* it used to be".
Do Mori is one of the oldest and most picturesque
eateries in the Rialto market and worth a visit if only
for its historical interest.
Try a *saltimbocca al sugo* or a *francobollo* (literally,
"postage stamp"), a tiny, well-filled *tramezzino*,
and wash it down with an ombra of unbottled wine.

ae Do Marie [€ 30] 🍴☀

+39 041 2960424, Castello 3129, Calle dell'Olio, closed Sunday

Ae Do Marie has recently re-opened. The new version is very
different from the *bacaro* it has replaced. For now, it offers
inexpensive midday meals for local workers and a more
ambitious evening menu for everyone else.
We'll be monitoring progress.

Elio 🍷☀

+39 041 5203190, San Polo 317, Campo de le Becarie ● 6.30 am–7.30 pm, closed Monday

Busy from the moment it opens, Elio is a favourite with local
fishmongers. The *oste* enjoys inventing new names for his constantly
changing *tramezzino* fillings. Try a *scoasse de marcà* ("market floor
sweepings" of prawns, roast pork and red-leaf chicory), *magnar de
'na volta* ("old-time eating" with chicken gizzard and grilled
peppers), or a *papussa dea nona* ("granny's slipper").

Fiaschetteria Toscana [€ 70]
🍴 🍷 ☀ ♡

+39 041 5285281, Cannaregio 5719,
Salizada San Giovanni Grisostomo,
closed Tuesday and Monday morning

If you want to impress someone
special, then bring your guest
to the Fiaschetteria Toscana.
"You can't go wrong", as they say.
Among the secrets of the
restaurant's success are its
understated but very elegant
ambience and great Venetian
meat and fish dishes, prepared with first quality ingredients
and presented on a balanced menu that reflects the season.
The mixed fry of monkfish, squid, soft-shell crab and cuttlefish
is to die for. Nor will you easily forget Mariuccia's sweet trolley,
which offers honey and hazelnut parfait in a chocolate timbale,
or the pears in flaky pastry with fruit sauce. The cellar is Albino's
pride and joy, with 900 wines to choose from. But if you insist
on ordering your personal favourite, you will have to cross
swords with Roberto, Claudio and Lollo.

the Fiddler's Elbow 🍷 ☀

+39 041 5239930, Cannaregio 3847, Corte dei Pali
⏺ 5 pm–12 pm, open all week

The Fiddler's Elbow is a lively pub, the haunt of young
people from abroad and multilingual students. You'll find
them all here of an evening, chatting like old friends.
In summer, the small open court is a great place to sit
outside until late, slowly sipping a beer.
Pay at the bar (€ 2.10). There's no surcharge for sitting down,
which is rare, if not unique, in Venice.
Recently, *panini* have been on offer, as well as the much admired
draught Guinness, Kilkenny, Harp, Beck's and Cashel's cider.
Ah, that first refreshing mouthful!

Fiore 🍷

+39 041 5235310, San Marco 3461, Calle de le Botteghe
⏺ 9 am–10.30 pm closed Tuesday

Fiore is an *osteria*-trattoria. Don't confuse
it with Da Fiore, which is in a completely
different location – and price band.
Head straight for the busy bar, where
you will find meatballs, *nerveti* with onion,
folpeti with celery, *luganega* and many other
tempting *cicheti*.

da Fiore [€ 110] 🍴 🍷

+39 041 721308, San Polo 2202a, Calle del Scaleter, closed Sunday and Monday

One of Venice's very finest restaurants, Da Fiore is in the top bracket, not just for price but also for quality of cuisine, its discreetly elegant decor, the great and the good who dine here, but above all for a *je ne sais quoi* that sets it apart from the rest and ensures a prominent place in all the major guides. From the list of *antipasti*, we suggest marinated scampi or salmon, *canoce*, *garusoli*, boiled *moscardini* and *schie* with soft *polenta*, or a fish risotto. Then try a tempting *secondo*, such as baked turbot in a crust of potatoes, bass with vegetables *al cartoccio* or, depending on the time of year, a mixed fry of *canestreli*, *moeche*, scampi or squid. The desserts are all made on the premises. Naturally, the wine list, with its 500 entries, is as impressive as you would expect.

Fontana [€ 39] 🍴 ☀

+39 041 715077, Cannaregio 1102, Fondamenta di Cannaregio
○ 6 pm–11 pm, closed Sunday

Swept by the north lagoon winds, between the Ponte delle Guglie and the Ghetto, is a long-established *osteria* that sells unbottled Veneto and Friulian wine. Its working-class clientele meet here for a chat, or to enjoy the cool breezes at the tables that appear on the *fondamenta* at the first sign of spring. For the past few years, it has also functioned as a small but well-run trattoria, where you can sample spaghetti with eel, *granseola* risotto or *gnocchi* with turbot and courgettes.

al Fontego dei Pescaori [€ 47] 🍴 🍷 ☀ 💳

+39 041 5200538, Cannaregio 3711, Sotoportego del Tagiapiera, closed Tuesday

Bare brick walls, wooden furniture, a welcoming atmosphere and neat tables set the tone in this former residence and warehouse, with its portico on the canal and small courtyard to the rear. Fish dominates the menu, here and there with an oriental flavour or dressed with aromatic herbs, accompanied by estuary-grown vegetables (shrimp and artichoke salad, *granseola* and asparagus tips, risotto of *bruscandoli* and scampi, tagliolini with wild asparagus and *bevarasse*), but there is also space for meat, such as tagliata (thin slices) of beef, baked guinea-fowl or stuffed duck in *peverada* sauce.

Frary's Bar [€ 25] 🍴🍷

+39 041 720050, San Polo 2559, Fondamenta dei Frari, closed Tuesday

At last, a place that serves good Arab and Greek cuisine.

The menu is reassuring, with falafel (fried chickpea balls), dolmades (rice wrapped in vine leaves), tzaziki, hummus, souvlaki (spicy chicken on a skewer), mansaf (Bedouin rice with chicken, almonds and yoghurt), couscous vegetarian style, or with mutton, chicken or seafood (shrimp, octopus and squid), beef kebabs and mutton yiros. The pistachio, date, raisin and rosewater ice cream is delicious. Sahitain! Enjoy your meal! Sohitak! Cheers!

alla Frasca [€ 17/38] 🍴🍷☀️ 🔲

+39 041 5285433, Cannaregio 5176, Corte della Carità, closed Thursday

This small but irresistible *osteria* has undergone yet another change of management. It is located in a lovely *campiello*, tucked away in the maze of *calli* near Fondamente Nuove.

The attractively priced midday *primi* and *secondi* for hungry locals are replaced by more expensive traditional dishes in the evening.

Gislon [€ 27] 🍴🍷

+39 041 5223569, San Marco 5424, Calle della Bissa ● 9 am–9.30 pm, closed Monday evening

All the delights of the Venetian kitchen – and more – lie before you on the long counter. Enjoy them while standing at one

of the wall-mounted shelves or sitting in comfort in the first-floor restaurant. There's meat, fish or vegetable *pasticcio*, soups, risottos, octopus salad, boiled vegetables, *baccalà*, either *mantecata* or *alla vicentina*, and breaded veal cutlets. Gislon is the perfect place for a quick meal at lunchtime. When you have elbowed your way to the bar, you can sample the *mozzarella in carrozza* with anchovies or ham, and the *arancini*.

Harry's Bar [€ 160] 🍸 ♟ 🛎 ♡

+39 041 5285777, San Marco 1323, Calle Vallaresso
● 10.30 am–11 pm, open all week

Arrigo Cipriani is not just a very superior *oste*. He is also one of Venice's opinion-makers, a man who ruminates and writes – never predictably – on life and civilisation in general. The restaurants reflect the man. These are ambiences that others attempt to imitate in vain for it is no easy task to communicate luxury with a perfect sense of proportion and effortless understatement. Harry's Bar instantly puts guests at their ease. Relaxed and informal, it also contrives to maintain an aura of absolute exclusivity. One wonders whether Arrigo is, as well as a world-class host, a talent scout of genius. His staff – and he has lots – are amazingly cordial yet professional, impeccable yet never stuffy. This costs but Arrigo, who is a bit of a political animal, has his own marketing strategy. He believes that "everything has its price" and manages to maintain the loyalty of a Venetian hard core – lawyers, university professors, aristocrats and petty nobility – ensuring that Harry's Bar is never in danger of being taken over by wealthy *foresti*. Prices, of course, are wallet-crippling. Some of the offerings could be matched by many other Venetian restaurants, but the legend lives on in Harry's classic risotto primavera, *carpaccio* and curried dory with pilaf. If all this is beyond your budget, then indulge yourself with a cocktail at the bar. Sip a Bellini or a Martini on one of Harry's high stools and see how the other half drinks.

Harry's Dolci [€ 110] 🍸 ♟ 🛎 ☀ ♡

+39 041 5224844–5208337, Giudecca 773, Fondamenta San Biagio ● 10 am–11.30 pm (from April to October), closed Monday and Tuesday

It may be the terrace of Harry's Bar but Harry's Dolci has a very different personality. There's no better spot for a lovers' tryst before a romantic trip in a motorboat, or waterbus, to the far end of the Giudecca. Relax on the *fondamenta*, admiring the beauty of the view while you assess one of the more ambitious cocktails. Or enjoy a plate of baked tagliolini with ham, turkey in tuna sauce, a lemon meringue or Harry's legendary chocolate cake.

da Ignazio [€ 47] 🍴🍷☀🔍

+39 041 5234852, San Polo 2749, Calle dei Saoneri, closed Saturday

After picking your way through a bewildering maze of narrow *calli*, you will emerge into a bright, spacious, pergola-bedecked courtyard where, weather permitting, you can enjoy your meal. Locals are very fond of Da Ignazio, partly because of the informal yet faultless service and partly because the menu is solidly traditional. Prominent are fan shell scallops, *canoce*, *granseole*, risottos and fish – baked, fried and above all grilled.

l'Incontro [€ 45] 🍴☀🔍

+39 041 5222404, Dorsoduro 3062, Rio Terà Canal, closed Monday and Tuesday morning

Near Campo Santa Margherita, there is a long established and much loved eatery, famous for Luciano's Sardinian specialties, artichoke botargo, rabbit salad, culingiones (large ravioli with saffron, ricotta and pecorino cheese, aromatised with orange peel), frattau bread (based on carasau – literally "music paper" – bread, soaked with hot stock, and arranged in alternate layers with tomato and pecorino sauce with a poached egg on top), oven roast suckling pig with myrtle and, to finish, Luciano's irresistible seadas (large sweet ravioli filled with fresh pecorino, fried and coated with honey while still hot). And when the Sardinian specialties are out of season, try the delicious orecchiette or trofie pasta (made on the premises) with fresh vegetable sauces or the excellent *tagliata* (thin slices) of beef.

- 40

da Lele 🍷

Santa Croce 183, Campo dei Tolentini ● 6 am–2 pm and 4 pm–8 pm, closed Saturday afternoon and Sunday

Little more than a hole in the wall, Da Lele has a regular clientele of lecturers, students and administrative staff from the nearby school of architecture.

A Venetian institution, it also serves commuters from the mainland, who drop in for a glass of Merlot, Cabernet or Raboso (€ 0.50). Genuine *Clinton* arrives in November and quickly runs out. When it's gone, it's gone.

The *panini* are also the real McCoy (€ 0.80), with *pancetta* and small artichokes, spicy salami and asiago mezzano cheese, lard from Valle d'Aosta (we are heartily fed up with Colonna clones), roast pork or mortadella.

alla Madonna [€ 44]

+39 041 5223824, San Polo 594, Calle de la Madonna,
closed Wednesday

A tried, trusted and well-loved restaurant right
next to the Rialto bridge. Commodious
and always crowded, it caters for large
numbers of diners with white tablecloths and
fast, attentive service. The kitchen is unfailingly
good and, thanks to the high turnover, offers
a great range of fish and meat dishes at prices
unmatchable elsewhere.

On the menu are *sarde in saor*, *granseola*, *folpeti*, fish soup,
schie, eels, fried squid, cuttlefish, grilled red mullet and lobster
with mayonnaise, as well as lasagne *pasticcio*, tripe, Venetian
style liver, roast chicken, breaded veal cutlets, grilled veal chops
and more, all accompanied by seasonal vegetables.
It's the perfect spot for a large family gathering – when
you just know that everyone will want something different.

dalla Marisa [€ 27]

+39 041 720211, Cannaregio 652b, Fondamenta San Giobbe, closed Sunday, Monday and Wednesday evenings

Dalla Marisa used to be just a no-nonsense trattoria for the residents of San Giobbe and one
or two adventurous diners from the other side of the Cannareggio
fondamenta. Today, it has been discovered by *foresti* and features
in many guides. Fame has not changed it, though, and Marisa
continues to do what she knows best. The scion of a dynasty
of *becheri* (butchers), she offers an authentic, meat-based menu.
Duck sauces grace huge plates of tagliatelle, risotto with *secoe*,
sguassetti alla bechera (beef in gravy), mixed boiled meats,
tripe and succulent venison ragouts with seasonal vegetables.
Everything is absolutely fresh and cooked to order.
The only problem is finding a table so book well in advance.
At the end of your
meal, you will be
given a "doggy bag"
with your leftovers.

'e Masaniello [€ 63] 🍴 🍷 ☀

041 5209003, San Marco 2801, Campo Santo
Stefano, closed Tuesday

A true Neapolitan bar-cum-
restaurant with a delicious Mediterranean menu. There's scapece, or marinade, of shrimp and
rocket, parmigiana of courgettes without tomato, pappardelle pasta with baby squid, boiled
shellfish with Amalfi lemon sauce, superb salads (€ 11) and sweets made on the premises.
It's all here in one of Venice's main *campi*.

alla Mascareta 🍷 🍶

+39 041 5230744, Castello 5183, Calle Lunga Santa Maria Formosa ● 7 pm–2 am, closed Wednesday and Thurday

One of Venice's cosiest *enoteche*. In addition to the bar area, there is a very quiet, warm room with
attractive tables and old sideboards. Here, the genial female *osti,* will welcome and advise you,
allowing you to taste in peace. Good wine, particularly if there are enough of you to justify uncorking
a bottle, served in the right glass can be accompanied by a plate of cold meats, cheeses or *crostini*.
After dinner, you can enjoy a sweet wine with petit fours. Your visit could be an opportunity to get to
know the wines of the Veneto, and perhaps buy a bottle to take home.

Try a delicately aromatic Bianco di Custoza, a young
Soave, an up-front Cabernet from Pramaggiore, a richly
scented Sauvignon from the Colli Euganei
or a sweet Recioto.

Mirai [€ 50] 🍴 🎴

+39 041 2206517, Cannaregio 227,Lista di Spagna,
open evenings only, closed Monday

A recently opened Japanese
restaurant that offers a wide range
of raw and cooked dishes, with a few
surprises. If there are two of you,
sit at the counter and watch how
the food is prepared.

Sample the highly recommended
sashimi, raw fish –
usually salmon, tuna or
bass – served with soya
sauce and wasabi, the
hot Japanese
horseradish.

You'll find round or
rectangular sushi of
boiled rice wrapped up
with various ingredients
and norimaki, similar to sushi but cylindrical.
To drink, there's sake or Japanese beer.
Hadakaimasu (enjoy your meal). Kampai (cheers).

Mistrà [€ 28/43] 🍴

+39 041 5220743, Giudecca 212a, closed Monday evening and Tuesday

Disembark at the Redentore, turn your back on the city and head down a narrow *calli* that will take
you to the magical lights of the south lagoon. On the first floor of an abandoned industrial building
with a panoramic outside staircase, you will find a well-lit restaurant with a cuisine blending
Ligurian with Venetian. The midday menu is brief and inexpensive, for the benefit of local dock
workers (pasta with bolognese sauce and mustard steak). In the evening, these are joined by nicely
prepared fish and other delights, such as octopus and potato salad, trofie pasta with pesto,
spaghetti *al cartoccio* and fish baked or grilled in salt.

Monaco–Gran Canal [€ 85] 🍷🍽🍴☀

+39 041 5200211, San Marco 1325, Calle Vallaresso, open all week

This stylish and justly famous restaurant adjoins the
hotel of the same name. We'll have to wait until
summer 2003 for the re-opening of the magnificent terrace facing the Salute church, right where
the Canal Grande meets the glorious waterfront of the Bacino di San Marco. For now, the massive
renovation effort gives us a unique opportunity to dine, or just have a drink, in the theatre of the
Ridotto. In the eighteenth century, it was a celebrated gaming house for the nobility, as well as
artfully disguised commoners. The Venetian and international cuisine is equal to the exalted
surroundings. Try the salmon and swordfish tartare, grilled fish or beef and, to round off the meal,
apple tatin (upside-down tart). Live piano music in the evening (except Tuesday).

los Murales [€ 24] 🍽🍷🍴☀

+39 041 5230004, Giudecca 70, Fondamenta Zitelle ● 9.30 am–12 pm, closed Wednesday

Disembark at the Zitelle and here you are. Los Murales is very economical, despite its marvellous
view. This bar with Mexican food has a tasty range of maize tortillas, vegetables, cheese, beans,
beef and chicken. Try the arroz valenciana (rice casserole), burritos, tacos or fajitas, then finish
with a crema catalana.

ai Nomboli ☗ ☀

+39 041 5230995, San Polo 2717, Calle Goldoni
● 7 am–9 pm, closed Saturday and Sunday

Great *panini* and *tramezzini* with an
astonishing range of fillings, plus good
old-fashioned courtesy, make this a
favourite stop. Choose from asparagus,
roast pork, gorgonzola, roast beef and
many more. There's something for
everyone. If you're lucky, there might
be a free table outside where you can
watch passersby on their way to and
from Campo San Polo and San Tomà.

al Nono Risorto [€ 36] ☖ ☀ ☕

041 5241169, Santa Croce 2338, sottoportego de la Siora Bettina
● 12–14.30 e 19–24, closed Wednesday and Thurday Morning

Young, friendly management, a spacious dining
area, good prices and late closing make the
"Resurrected Grandad" the trattoria of choice
for many Venetian thirtysomethings, especially
in summer. The large wistaria-shaded garden
features gravel underfoot and heavy oak tables.
Good pizzas (€ 5–8), salads and a Venetian menu.   45 –

Olandese Volante ☗ ☀ ☕

+39 041 5289349, Castello 5658, Campo San Lio
● 11 am–1 am, closed Sunday morning

A sandwich and beer bar with a generous
seating area outside where you can enjoy the
cool of the evening, nibbling crisps, *panini*
or a salad until late.
Venetian cooking is also available at midday.

Oliva Nera [€ 57] 🍴 🐚 ☀

+39 041 5222170, Castello 3417, Salizada dei Greci, closed Wednesday

The Oliva Nera is a friendly *osteria* with a few tables in the *calle*. Many of the diners are passing tourists – we're very near San Giorgio dei Greci – who pop in for a tasty snack. There are plenty to choose from, including octopus and potato salad, stuffed courgette flowers, fan shell scallops and porcini mushrooms, lobster and scampi soup, pasta with broccoli and mussels, *gnocchetti* with shellfish sauce and some of the classic Venetian dishes. There are also meat options, like beef *tagliata* (thin slices) with caper and rosemary sauce or chicken with *vellutata* (cream) of asparagus. The desserts are good and the interesting wine list has over 100 entries.

al Pantalon [€ 36] 🍴 🍷

+39 041 710849, Dorsoduro 3958, Calle del Scaleter
🕐 10.30 am–2.30 pm and 6.30 pm–10 pm, closed Sunday (*see next entry*)

alla Patatina [€ 36] 🍴 🍷

+39 041 5237238, San Polo 2741, Ponte San Polo 🕐 10.30 am–3 pm and 6 pm–10 pm, closed Sunday

It's amazing how the unruffled owners of Alla Patatina and its twin Al Pantalon have managed to conserve the 1950s atmosphere of these eateries, with no concessions to passing food fads. The formula is tried, tested and immutable. There are no exceptions and the watchword is "feed 'em". The counter is always well stocked and the kitchen ceaselessly turns out tasty, nutritious fare, to be washed down with vigorous wines (dieters should take note). Regular as clockwork, students, building workers and commuters troop in, united by hunger and their robust digestion.

On the menu will be spaghetti with cockles, crab or tuna, fish risottos, fried cuttlefish and *baccalà mantecato*.

At the counter, you'll find meatballs in gravy, fried vegetables, *sarde in saor*, *nerveti*, *museto* with *polenta*, *bovoleti*, *spiensa*, courgette flowers in batter, and, of course, the skewers of fried potato slices that have made the eatery in Calle Saoneri famous. The other "branch", Al Pantalon, is near to the university at Ca' Foscari. At graduation time, it is busy putting on lavish buffets for new graduates, their admiring relatives and other guests.

al Paradiso Perduto [€ 43] 🍷 ⚲ ☼

+39 041 720581, Cannaregio 2540, Fondamenta de la Misericordia
● 7 pm–2 am (open midday and evening Saturday and Sunday), closed Tuesday and Wednesday

A big boisterous bar with informal service and a clientele of young people and Venice's last surviving hippies, Al Paradiso Perduto is a one-off. Live music, often jazz, on Sundays and Mondays. Snackers sip *ombre*, Cividale wines and draught beers while tucking into *bigoli in salsa*, fried fish and *polenta*, cuttlefish *in tecia* and assorted vegetables.

la Perla [€ 34] 🍷 ⚲

+39 041 5285175, Cannaregio 4615,
Rio Terà dei Franceschi, closed Sunday

This large eatery may not have memorable decor but you'll always find noisy groups of friends quaffing beer at the tables. Good pizzas (€ 5–8) with a wide range of fine quality toppings. There are also one or two "over the toppings", such as sausage and chips, pumpkin cream and shrimp. Who'd eat a pizza like that?

da Pinto 🍷 ☼

+39 041 5224599, San Polo 367, Campo de le Becarie ● 10 am–3 pm and 6 pm–9.30 pm, closed Monday

Da Pinto was one of Rialto's oldest *osterie* – it's been selling wine from Puglia since 1890 – serving the fish market. Sadly, the tables in Campo de le Becarie are increasingly occupied by tourists, who have inevitably influenced the food. Nowadays, it's all lasagne, pizza and cannelloni!
Go straight to the bar, where you can console yourself with an *ombra* and some grilled *folpeto* or a *crostino* with *baccalà*.

al Ponte ♟

+39 041 5286157, Cannaregio 6378, Ponte del Cavallo ● 6 am–10 pm, closed Sunday

The new managers at Al Ponte have managed to retain former customers, also attracting new clients and the occasional tourist, who is immediately adopted and offered friendly advice. At the counter or at one of the tables, savour the delicious small *panini* with *pancetta steccata* (pork belly matured between two pieces of wood), salami, beef and peppers, mortadella or excellent *baccalà mantecato*, accompanied by a glass of Merlot, Raboso del Piave or Cabernet Franc.

ai Postali ♟

Santa Croce 821, Fondamenta di Rio Marin
● 8 am–3 pm and 5 pm–2 am, closed Sunday

– 48 It's relaxing to sit at the tables on the edge of the *fondamenta* with a gin and tonic or *spritz*, and something to eat, as you watch the world drift gently past.

al Portego [€ 25] 🍴♟♡

+39 041 5229038, Castello 6015, Calle de la Malvasia ● 10 am–3 pm and 6 pm–10 pm, closed Sunday

By a quiet *portego* between San Lio and Santa Marina, there's a small and cosy *osteria* with wood everywhere – ceiling, walls, bar, tables and barrels. The windows are curtained and there is a separate dining area for those who want to sit and eat in peace. The *cicheti* include meat and tuna balls, fried vegetables, *folpeti* and *crostini*. If you prefer something hot, there's *bigoli in salsa*, fish risottos, *pasta e fasioi*, Venetian-style liver or *museto* with *polenta*.

al Prosecco 🍷🍴☀♡

+39 041 5240222, Santa Croce 1503, San Giacomo
dall'Orio ☉ 8 am–10.30 pm, closed Sunday

There's nothing nicer than to sit in the shade in the
lively Campo di San Giacomo dall'Orio to enjoy the antics of the dogs and children.
And it's even more satisfying if you have a glass of good Prosecco. The hard-working young owners
of Al Prosecco can give you this, which is why they attract customers from all over Venice.
There's a good selection of cheeses and cold meats (a plate for two costs € 10–20), *crostini*, seven
or eight wines by the glass and plenty of bottles. On Saturdays, you can enjoy oysters and raw fish.
The room inside is a pleasant refuge on wet afternoons.

49 –

Quadri [€ 100] 🍽🍷🍴☀

+39 041 5222105, Piazza San Marco 120 ☉ 9 am–12 pm, closed Monday

Access to the ground-floor rooms of Quadri, decorated with pastel-coloured stuccoes and ornate
mirrors, is under the arches of the Procuratie Vecchie. Above, the first-floor windows look onto
Piazza San Marco and the Basilica. After all, it won't bankrupt you to indulge in breakfast, or even a
modest evening meal, in one of the world's most breathtakingly beautiful settings. It's not just your
eyes that enjoy the experience: the food is excellent. There are delicate fish or shellfish *antipasti*,
superb *primi* – risotto with *bruscandoli*, chestnut flour *gnocchetti* with duck sauce, creamed borlotti
beans and mussels with leeks – fish or meat *secondi* redolent of aromatic herbs and spices, as well
as a number of vegetarian dishes. Adriano has been running the restaurant successfully for many
years and periodically organises tastings.

Quatro Feri [€ 35] 🍽 🍴

041 5206978, Dorsoduro 2754a, Calle Lunga San Barnaba, closed Sunday

Located at the end of the calle that leads from Campo San Barnaba to San Sebastian, the Quatro Feri has the authentic look of an old-style Venetian *osteria*. It combines oak tables, paper placemats and friendly service with a management style that focuses on quality and fresh ingredients. The trays of traditional specialties are on the counter (octopus salad, *folpeti, baccalà mantecato* and a fine range of vegetables).
The kitchen produces good vegetable and shellfish *primi* (pumpkin *gnocchi* with prawns and baby broccoli or spaghettini with swordfish and courgette flowers), as well as grilled fish and the house specialty, tuna *in saor*.
Fair selection of wines.

il Refolo [€ 48] 🍴 🍷 ☼ 🍕

+39 041 5240016, Santa Croce 1459, Campiello del Piovan ◑ 12 am–3.30 pm and 6 pm–12 pm, closed Monday and Tuesday

You'll think you've walked into a painting. This is one of the prettiest spots in Venice.
Il Refolo looks unassuming but inside, you'll find lots of pleasant surprises. Under new management, it continues to make pizzas but they are much more sophisticated than before. They're also pricier (€ 6–12).
You can choose from a small but tempting menu that includes marinated salmon, *mozzarella in carrozza* with *misticanza*, tuna hamburger and other unusual titbits, fresh salads and selected cheeses. The beers are also good.
In short, it's a spot for those who demand quality – and are prepared to pay for it.

da Remigio [€ 44]

+39 041 5230089, Castello 3416, Salizada dei Greci, closed Monday evening and Tuesday

Da Remigio is a firm favourite with Venetians who like affordable prices, white tablecloths, fast but not distracted service and, above all, fresh fish simply prepared. There's *canoce*, boiled *folpeti*, grilled razor shells, spaghetti with *caparossoli*, or alla busara (with a paprika, garlic and brandy-based sauce), risottos, soups and, of course, fried and grilled fish.

In a nutshell, this is where to come for a great fish meal, at a price that won't spoil your digestion.

Ribò [€ 57] ※

+39 041 5242486, Santa Croce 158, Rio del Gaffaro, closed Wednesday

A well-lit, cheerful eatery with a sophisticated menu of light fries and combinations that are no longer fashionable, such as *granseola* pie with potatoes and French beans in oil and lemon, scampi and artichoke risotto, *tagliata* (thin slices) of tuna with aromatic herbs and marinated cauliflower, fish soup, steamed eel with peas and a few meat dishes.

Rioba [€ 40]

+39 041 5244379, Cannaregio 2553, Fondamenta della Misericordia, closed Monday

Bare brick walls, wooden beams and plain tables greet you in this recently opened *osteria*.
Well-lit and welcoming, it is named after Rioba, one of the four "Moorish merchants", the curiously
beturbaned eponymous marble figures in the nearby Campo. The menu is limited but scrupulously
prepared, from the *schie con la polentina al saor*, to the spaghetti with lobster and the various –
very fresh – fish *secondi*. You'll also see one or two meat dishes, like fillet steak or rabbit.
In summer, you can sit at one of the tables on the *fondamenta*.

Rivetta [€ 39]

+39 041 5287302, Castello 4625, Ponte San Provolo, ● 10 am–22 pm, closed Monday

A traditional trattoria, much frequented by the local gondoliers. Despite the crowds, the Rivetta
manages to offer a fine range of *cicheti* – *sarde in saor*, *latti di seppia* and roast potatoes – on the
counter for those on their way in or out of the trattoria. At table, you can sample the usual Venetian
meat or fish dishes, as well as pasta with
bolognese sauce or a *cotoletta alla milanese*.

Rivetta ♟♡

Santa Croce 637a, Calle Sechera
● 8.30 am–9.30 pm, closed Sunday

Wine here is served from the
demijohn (an *ombra* costs € 0.60),
to wash down crostini with *baccalà* or
gorgonzola, hot *panini* with *sopressa*,
salami, *pancetta*, grilled eggplant and
courgettes, salad and a never-ending
stream of conversation from the
landlord and the drinking public.
Rivetta is a genuine neighbourhood
bacaro, not far from the Tolentini
church and the railway station.

la Rivista [€ 50] ♟♟

+39 041 2401425, Dorsoduro 979a, Calle
Larga Pisani ● 7.30 am–11 pm, closed Monday

Originally conceived as a wine and
cheese bar, La Rivista is fast becoming
a favourite in a part of Venice where
good eateries are hard to come by.
It offers a connoisseur's wine list,
with as many as twenty wines available   53 –
by the glass, and an interesting
selection of Italian cheeses (bagòss,
murazzano, barbatasso, murianengo and others),
as well as a tasty menu. You'll find potato and black
truffle ravioli with artichoke and *vongole veraci*, back
of suckling pig with cucumber and tomato salad in
fresh coriander sauce or cherry soup with traditional
balsamic vinegar and plain ice cream.

Ruga Rialto [€ 33] ♟♟☼

+39 041 5211243, San Polo 692, Ruga Rialto
● 11 am–3 pm and 6 pm–12 pm, open all week

A capacious osteria for large, noisy groups.
There are a few *cicheti* at the bar and a brief
menu of unambitious traditional food. The
main reason for coming is the *simpatia* of the
three young *osti*, Marco, Giorgio and Giorgio.
The trio love to organise themed evenings and
there is live music on Fridays.

ai Rusteghi 🍷🐚☀

+39 041 5232205, San Marco 5513, Campiello del Tentor ● 9.30 am–3 pm
and 5 pm–8.30 pm, closed Saturday (only in summer) and Sunday

Ai Rusteghi has moved into the *campiello* on the left, a
little further on from its former site. It has also acquired
some outside tables. The *ombre* are good and served in
suitable glasses. The *panini*, though, are perfection –
small, soft and with more than thirty different fillings.
Choose from chicken salad, lard and rosemary,
roast pork and chicory, egg and asparagus, shrimp and porcini
mushrooms, and more besides.
The *osti* live up to their name and can be decidedly "rustic".
Particularly if you try to light up a cigarette.

Sahara [€ 26] 🍴☀🍷

+39 041 721077, Cannaregio 2519, Fondamenta de la Misericordia
● 12 am–2.30 pm and 7 pm–2 am (in summer open evenings only),
closed Monday (only in winter)

This *fondamenta* is a popular meeting place, especially
on a summer's evening. It is crowded with places to eat, all with
a table or two outside but the Sahara is the only ethnic eatery
worth mentioning, particularly since it has moderate prices
and serves meals until late.
So let's dive in and explore the menu of strange-sounding
Arab and Syrian specialties. Falafel are small fried balls of
chickpea, flavoured with coriander and onion; magluba is rice
with eggplant, minced beef, almonds and pine nuts served
with yoghurt; and there are also meat kebabs.
Couscous comes with meat, vegetables or fish to order.
In the kitchen, Mouaffak runs things and wife Rita serves at the

tables. The – at times, incredibly slow – service is part of the place's mystique for almost everything

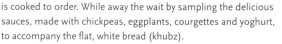

is cooked to order. While away the wait by sampling the delicious
sauces, made with chickpeas, eggplants, courgettes and yoghurt,
to accompany the flat, white bread (khubz).

San Basilio [€ 46] 🍴🍷☀

+39 041 5210028, Dorsoduro 1406, Fondamenta Zattere ● 9 am–10.30 pm, closed Sunday

When Venetians want to feel they're on holiday on a warm spring day,
they book a table here on the *fondamenta* facing the Giudecca
canal and the Mulino Stucky.
The San Basilio offers a friendly welcome and a traditional menu,
including *spaghetti al nero di seppia* (in cuttlefish ink) and fried
scampi and squid.

San Marco [€ 49] ♟🍴🥂🍷

+39 041 5285242 San Marco 1610, Frezzeria,
◔ 10.30 am–11.30 pm, closed Sunday

Here's a little gem. Four young partners, all
with catering experience and all keen as
mustard, have taken over a neglected trattoria in one of Venice's
most central *calli*, restored it tastefully and transformed it into an
osteria-enoteca. Word of mouth among friends and well-wishers
ensured a triumphant opening. The innovative menu is based on
traditional flavours, such as crab salad with rosemary, scampi and
courgette flower risotto or herb-baked fillet of sea bream, and
supported by a good wine list. You can also linger at the bar,
nibbling the cheeses and cold meats and
watching people in the *calle* hurry past the large windows.

Santa Marina [€ 59] 🍷🍴🥂☀

+ 39 041 5285239, Castello 5911, Campo Santa Marina, closed Sunday and Monday at midday

Two couples have joined forces on this upmarket adventure: Agostino, Betty and Caterina run the
kitchen and Danilo looks after the tables. After a shaky start, they have earned the respect of many
local gourmets. The extravagantly named dishes are beautifully presented and very, very good.
Scampi in leek and ginger *saor*, *folpeti* with Tropea onion, orange peel and balsamic vinegar, raw
lobster and mignonette pie, cream of borlotti beans with spicy tuna morsels or grilled skewers
of fish and shellfish with smoked lard can be followed by the very popular hot chocolate pie or the
apple pie with cinnamon ice cream. For something more refreshing, try the basil sorbet with wild
berries. The wine list is tempting and the outside tables are very pleasant.

da Sergio [€ 16] ⊸🍴🍷🔍

+39 041 5285153, Castello 5870a, Calle del Dose, closed Saturday evening and Sunday

It's like eating at your auntie's. Angelo waits table while Mimma is in the kitchen, rustling up minestrone, *pasticcio*, pasta, roasts, steaks, roast potatoes and buttered spinach. Da Sergio is extremely popular with working people from the Campo Santa Maria Formosa and Santa Marina area who are tired of lunching on *panini*. Here, they can find homestyle cooking at very competitive prices. The bar also flaunts a fine range of meatballs, *sarde in saor*, *nerveti* and *folpeti*. The kitchen is closed in the evening.

il Sole sulla Vecia Cavana [€ 64] 🍴🍾📷

+39 041 5287106, Cannaregio 4624, Rio Terà Santi Apostoli, closed Monday

Not many eaters-out have discovered Il Sole sulla Vecia Cavana yet so you can usually find a table. Stefano took over a few years ago and restored it carefully, adding a "sole", or sun, as his personal signature. A man of the world who has travelled far and wide, Stefano has imbued the spacious restaurant with his extensive professional experience. Light and colour are used skilfully to frame the light, modern cuisine, based on the briefest of cooking times and extreme attention to ingredients. The menu includes some masterly re-interpretations of Venetian classics and other dishes that are creative but not excessively so. Try the fresh tuna tartare with piquant basil oil and teriyaki sauce (ginger, soya and sugar), *carpaccio* of sea perch and salmon with dill and pink pepper, or basil risotto and sautéed scallops. And what about honey ice cream with glazed pumpkin ravioli and mascarpone cheese to finish?
The wine list foregrounds Italian bottles, some of them hard to find.

Suziecafè ☕ ☀

+39 041 5227502, Dorsoduro 1527 ● 7 am–7 pm with live music until 2 am, closed Saturday and Sunday

A sandwich bar with plenty of tables outside. Suziecafè is always crowded with students, who come for the hot *tramezzini* and *panini*, as well as other offerings, such as asparagus risotto or pasta with vegetables. The scene is transformed in the evening, especially on Friday. There is live music in the *campo* and the party goes on until the wee small hours.

alle Testiere [€ 53] ⬤🍷🍶♡

+39 041 5227220, Castello 5801, Calle del Mondo Novo
● 12 am–3 pm and 7 pm–11 pm, closed Sunday and Monday

This tiny restaurant with a handful of tables has been a consistent success. Located in the *calle* that leads from Salizada di San Lio to Santa Maria Formosa, its secret is the blend of skill and enthusiasm Bruno and Luca bring to bear. In the kitchen, Bruno keeps an eagle eye on the quality of the ingredients. He lovingly prepares tiny *gnocchi* with baby squid in cinnamon, *caparossoli* sautéed with a hint of ginger, linguine with slivers of monkfish, tepid *granseola*, and fillet of dory with aromatic herbs in orange and lemon sauce.
The same fanatical attention is lavished on the desserts. Don't miss the pear, ricotta and chocolate pie, or the crema rosada, an ancient and now rediscovered recipe.
Luca is the wine man – his small selection reveals his thoughtful approach – and also supervises the cheese board. Some of the delights are escarun cuneese, verde di Montegalda vicentina and buccia di rospo, a hard to come by Tuscan pecorino cheese. Is that enough for you? Then be sure to book well ahead.

dai Tosi – Piccoli [€ 33] 🍴 🍷 ⚲ ☼

+39 041 5237102, Castello 738, Seco Marina
◉ 9.30 am–4 pm and 5 pm–11.30 pm, closed Wednesday

There are plenty of Venetians who appreciate Dai Tosi and its fine pizzas (to eat on the premises or take away: € 4-7). For a change, go for the spaghetti with scampi, squid, *mazzancolle* and vegetables. Note this address, and not just for the Biennale.

al Vecio Fritoin [€ 45] 🍴 🍷

+39 041 5222881, Santa Croce 2262, Calle della Regina
closed Monday

The delightfully enthusiastic Irina has been running Al Vecio Fritoin for several years. It was hard going at first but she is now beginning to enjoy the fruits of her efforts. The dining area couldn't be cosier or more inviting. The seasonal menu is traditional in focus, with one or two variations. There are grilled *canestrei* and fan shell scallops, fillet of sea bass with porcini mushrooms and lamb chops with vegetables. Wine list and cheese board are limited but carefully selected.

Vini da Arturo [€ 81] 🍴

+39 041 5286974, San Marco 3656, Calle dei Assassini
◉ 12.30 pm–2.30 pm and 7.30 pm–11 pm, closed Sunday (Saturday and Sunday in July)

So small some people call it the "vagone" (railway carriage), Vini da Arturo is nonetheless a very popular restaurant. For decades, Ernesto has been declaiming his unwritten and unchanging menu. Meat is the keynote, including Alessio's superb fillets of beef – with green pepper, strogonoff or voronoff – and the unique *braciola a la venexiana*, a chop for lovers of vinegar. The salads, served in small bowls, are irresistible, as are the eggplants *in saor*, spaghetti with chicory sauce and the couldn't-be-creamier *tiramisù* or the chocolate mousse.
Don't forget – credit cards are not accepted.

Vini da Gigio [€ 44]

+39 041 5285140, Cannaregio 3628a,
Fondamenta San Felice, closed Monday

Just off Strada Nuova, by the church of
San Felice, you'll find one of the best value
restaurants in Venice. Unfortunately, lots
of other people know about it, too,
so book well in advance.

The comfortable dining rooms and
small tables are ideal for small
groups of friends – no more than
four or five – who want to eat well
while conversing in an appropriately
leisurely fashion.

The service is exceptionally
courteous and serenely "Slow":
no one is going to rush you.

You can start with the impressive list
of Italian and international wines
and choose a menu to match or let

yourself be tempted by one of the meat or fish dishes – specialties include the raw fish *antipasto*,
baccalà croquettes, beef *carpaccio*, penne pasta with *granseola* or gorgonzola and pistachios,
gilled eel, fried fish, *masorino alla buranella* (Burano-style duck) and *fegato alla veneziana*.
Accompany your choice with a wine proposed by the staff, whose suggestions are always spot-on.
Make sure you try the puddings or a fruit crostata.
There's also a fine selection of grappas from the Veneto and Friuli.

ai Vini Padovani [€ 36]

+39 041 5236370, Dorsoduro 1280, Calle dei Cerchieri
● 10 am–10 pm, closed Saturday and Sunday

Although very central, Ai Vini Padovani is difficult to find
without a map or good directions. As you grope your
way through the maze of *calli* and courtyards behind
Calle de la Toletta, you are suddenly confronted by the
inviting prospect of this old neighbourhood *bacaro*.
The bar staff might encourage you to come in.
The locals might turn round to give you the once-over
and make a friendly comment, involving you in their
never-ending discussions. You'll feel right at home.
The counter always has a good stock of *cicheti*, or you
can sit in the wood-panelled dining area and eat some
cotechino sausage, shin of beef, veal in tuna sauce,
folpeti in salad or *baccalà*.

Vino Vino [€ 32/60] 🍴 🍷 🍶

+39 041 2417688, San Marco 2007a, Calle del Cafetier ● 10.30 am–12 pm, closed Tuesday

You could say that Vino Vino was opened as the wine bar of the Antico Martini restaurant, which supplies its raw materials and professional manner. The cuisine is Venetian and there are plenty of succulent snacks to accompany an astonishing number of wines by the glass. The range of meals is less expensive than the restaurant's but still good quality. There's octopus salad, *pasta e fasioi*, *baccalà*, either *alla vicentina* or *mantecato*, quail with *polenta*, roast rabbit or guinea fowl, veal stew, chine of suckling pig, beef stewed in Barolo or sautéed veal kidneys. Above all, Vino Vino is ideal if you want a quick meal without having to jostle with other diners at a narrow table.

Vitae 🍷 ☀ ♡

+39 041 5205205, San Marco 4118, Salizada San Luca
● 9 am–1.30 am, closed Saturday morning and Sunday

A marvellous refuge in the heart of the business area.
Modern, with plenty of tables outside, Vitae is a magnet for young professionals and more discriminating office workers in the Campo

San Luca area. You'll see them sipping expertly made aperitifs and cocktails as they sample the snacks and dips. Moito, caipirinha, margarita, cuba libre and daiquiris are popular. Equally good are the *crostini* and tempting little *tramezzini* with roast pork, chicory, olive, tuna, or vegetarian fillings.
At midday, there are bar meals of pork with boiled rice, chicken morsels with *castraure*, octopus salad with celery, cherry tomatoes and courgettes, as well as more exotic dishes like Spanish moquequa soup or a generous salad. Wash it down with a nice, cool glass of Prosecco.

Vivaldi [€ 52] 🍴 🍷 🥪

+39 041 5238185, San Polo 1457, Calle de la Madoneta
● 11 am–4 pm and 5 pm–11 pm, open all week

The umpteenth change of management seems to have done the trick for this attractive traditional eatery with its compact tables and wooden sideboards. The bar offers some Venetian specialties in the shape of abundant snacks and at table you can enjoy *pasta e fasioi*, spaghetti in cuttlefish ink, Venetian style liver or *tagliata* (thin slices) of beef with rosemary.

al Volto [€ 24] ♆ ▟ ※

+39 041 5228945, San Marco 4081, Calle Cavalli ● 10 am–2.30 pm
and 5 pm–10 pm, closed Sunday

There's a wide selection of labels on the shelves,
as well as on the ceiling. This is an uncompromising
osteria and there's even a table in the *calle*.
The counter is replete with marinated anchovies,
Greek style pilchards and baby artichokes, as well as
a few bar meals like *bigoli in salsa* or sausage risotto.

alla Zucca [€ 35] ◀▤ ▟ ▟ ※ ♡

+39 041 5241570, Santa Croce 1762, Ponte del Megio, closed Sunday

A classic. The quiet, well-lit dining area opens onto a few outside tables at the foot of the bridge.
Imagination – tempered with moderation – rules. Service is pleasingly informal and the cuisine is
inventive without being overdone. There are plenty of vegetables, some with a hint of the orient.
Try asparagus and potato soup, penne pasta with eggplant and Greek feta cheese, roast lamb with
fennel and pecorino cheese, mustard-baked rabbit with *polenta*, pumpkin flan with mature ricotta,
a vegetarian dish with rice and sesame, grilled breast of chicken with garlic and mint flavoured

tzatziki sauce, shin of veal on the bone with
peas, gratin of leeks with parmesan cheese,
pork in ginger with pilaf and, to finish your
meal, yoghurt ice cream with bilberries or
strawberries in Prosecco.
The brief wine list covers all of Italy and speaks
volumes for the energy that went into
compiling it.

... near Venice

If you want to explore the islands or
mainland, what Venetians disdainfully
call "the countryside", here are some
addresses from my little black book.
There aren't many but know the
eateries and enjoy eating there.

Ombre Rosse •

la Ost

• da Mar

• al Calice

• la Pergola

dall'Amelia •

• la Ragnatela

• da Conte

• da Caronte

da Ce

locanda Cipriani

da Romano

alla Maddalena   al Gatto Nero

Ca' Vignotto

Busa la Torre

all'Oasi

alle Vignole

Pachuka

Afrika

bar Trento

a Nane

Memo

islands

Burano

On Burano, there are two large, traditional trattorias with high ceilings, paintings on the walls, white tablecloths and families of Venetians – grandparents included – mingling with the tourists.
Both offer fresh fish and traditional, albeit occasionally soulless, cooking, with *antipasti* of shellfish from the lagoon, *gò* risotto and then a mixed fish fry or grill. Cast your vote.

da Romano [€ 52] 🍴 ☀

+39 041 730030, Piazza Galuppi 221, closed Sunday evening and Tuesday

The better known of the two establishments, located in the former lace school.

al Gatto Nero [€ 52] 🍴 ☀

+39 041 730120, Fondamenta Giudecca 88, closed Monday

After your meal, go out the back door and sit on the grass to enjoy the view.

Lido

We are not going to review the most famous restaurants. In summer, when we would most like to eat there, they are a tad overstretched with tourists sent by hotel porters.
Still, they are much quieter in winter.
Here are three very different, less pretentious eateries as an alternative.

Pachuka [€ 35] 🍴 ☀

+39 041 2420020, Spiaggia San Nicolò ● 8.30 am–12 pm, closed Tuesday (open all week in summer)

Head towards the embankment and beacon at the mouth of the San Nicolò harbour.
Between the grassy, dune-sheltered beach, covered with flowers in spring, and the holm oaks, you'll find this welcoming haven and its shady terrace. Self-service at midday, with a restaurant, pizzeria and disco in the evening. Have a final swim at sunset then, when the mosquitoes have disappeared, enjoy a fish fry with salad or grilled vegetables and glass of Prosecco or a draught beer.
Then trip the light fantastic.

Afrika [€ 35] 🍴 ☀

+39 041 5260186, Via Lazzaro Mocenigo 9, closed Tuesday

A trattoria for regulars and the occasional (hopelessy lost) tourist. Good mixed fish *antipasto*, a few pasta and rice options, then fried scampi and squid with a glass of cool Collio wine.

Bar Trento [€ 20] 🍴 ☀

+39 041 5265960, Via Sandro Gallo 82 ● 7 am–9 pm, closed Sunday

A genuine working-class *osteria* with a counter that is laden round the clock with *baccalà*, *folpeti*, *bovoleti*, *cotechino* sausage and *nerveti* with onion. The kitchen is open only at midday, when ravenous workers sit down to a substantial lunch under the bowers.
Evening meals are served during the cinema festival, when the Bar Trento is also open on Sundays.

Mazzorbo

alla Maddalena [€ 30] ⬤ 🍴 ☀

+39 041 730151, Mazzorbo 7 c, closed Thursday

It's worth the forty-minute waterbus ride to Alla Maddalena, right by the landing at Mazzorbo.
Alla Maddalena a traditional fish restaurant. In summer, you can sit under the bowers by the canal,
or relax in the quiet garden behind the restaurant. When the hunting season begins in September,
the menu includes feathered game, most of which is shot in the lagoon's fish farming *valli*,
and other winter favourites such as tripe and *pasta e fasioi*.

Murano

Busa la Torre [€ 42] 🍴 ☀

+39 041 739662, Campo Santo Stefano 3, open all week at midday only

The gentle, red-haired giant with the beard who greets you is called Lele and the *campo* where he will
entertain you is well-ventilated and very pleasant. The seasonal, fish-based menu boasts tagliatelle
with *canoce* or shrimp and *porcini* mushrooms, sea bass ravioli with *granseola* sauce and, of course,
Lele's legendary fried *moeche*.

Pellestrina

Three traditional, and fairly similar, establishments with little to choose between them.
All are large and often hired for christenings but, in summer, they are also patronised
by sailing parties looking for fresh fish.

da Celeste [€ 50] 🍴 ☀

+39 041 967355, Sestiere Vianelli 625b, closed Wednesday (open March to October)

The terrace must be the loveliest in the south lagoon.

da Nane [€ 58] 🍴 ☀

+39 041 5279100, San Piero in Volta 282, closed Monday (open April to November)

Another terrace on the lagoon and marvellous fish *pasticcio*.

da Memo [€ 54] 🍴 ☀

+39 041 5279125, San Piero in Volta 157 ⬤ 8am-12 pm closed Tuesday (open March to December)

This restaurant, its outside tables set in an attractive garden, stands on the Portosecco bend.

budget-threatening

al Bacareto [€ 48]
il Refolo [€ 48]
San Marco [€ 49]
Boccadoro [€ 50]
Mirai [€ 50]
la Rivista [€ 50]
da Celeste [€ 50]
Corte Sconta [€ 52]
Vivaldi [€ 52]
da Romano [€ 52]
al Gatto Nero [€ 52]
alle Testiere [€ 53] ◄■
da Memo [€ 54]
agli Alboretti [€ 55] ◄■
la Colombina [€ 57]
Oliva nera [€ 57]
Ribò [€ 57]
da Nane [€ 58]
Santa Marina [€ 59] ◄■
'e Masaniello [€ 63]
dall'Amelia [€ 63]
il Sole sulla Vecia Cavana [€ 64]
Acqua pazza [€ 68]
le Bistrot de Venise [€ 70]
Fiaschetteria Toscana [€ 70]
Locanda Cipriani [€ 74] ◄■
al Covo [€ 75]
Vini da Arturo [€ 81]

exclusive

Monaco – Gran Canal [€ 85] ◄■
Quadri [€ 100]
da Fiore [€ 110]
Harry's Dolci [€ 110]
la Cusina [€ 113]
Harry's Bar [€ 160]

A glossary of venexiàn (and Italian)

words ancient, old and new – an informal collection

Words included in the glossary are printed in italics in the text.

Syllables marked with an accent are stressed.

aciughèta (plural **aciughète**) anchovy

al cartòccio (standard Italian) baked in a sealed parcel of paper or foil

anguèla (plural **anguèle**) sand smelt (*Atherina presbyter*), common small lagoon fish

antipàsto (standard Italian: plural **antipàsti**) a starter

àmolo (plural **àmoli**) damson

ànara (plural **ànare**) duck

arancìno (standard Italian: plural **arancìni**) a ball of rice mixed with meat, ham or cheese, breaded and fried

armelìn (plural **armelìni**) apricot

articiòco (plural **articiòchi**) artichoke

asià spiny dogfish (*Squalus achantias*)

baccalà (standard Italian) dried cod

baccalà alla vicentìna dried cod cooked "Vicenza style", in tomatoes and olives

baccalà mantecato dried cod boiled, flaked then steamed and aromatised with garlic and parsley, then blended with oil until creamy

bàcaro (plural **bàcari**) see **osterìa**

bagìgi peanuts

baìcoli dry Venetian biscuits

baìcoli

baìcolo the young sea bass (*Dicentrarchus labrax*)

barbunsàl calf's chin, boiled with carrots and celery, then dressed with oil and vinegar when cold

barèna (plural **barène**) sandbank or land, normally submerged at high tide, with vegetation emerging above the water level

baùta (plural **baùte**) Carnival mask comprising a black hood and a lace cape

bechèr (plural **bechèri**) butcher

bevaràssa (plural **bevaràsse**) cockle (*Venus gallina*) or clam (US)

biancomangiàre (standard Italian) a milk pudding made with cornflour, cinnamon, pine nuts and zest of lemon

barbòn (plural **barbòni**) red mullet (*Mullus surmuletus* or *M. barbatus*)

bievaròl grocer's shop

bìgoli large coarse spaghetti, usually made with wholemeal wheat, used for **bìgoli in salsa** – the **salsa** is made by gently frying onions and anchovies. Once, this was a traditional meal on days of abstinence from meat

stracaganàse

spumìlia (plural **spumìlie**) meringue

squèro (plural **squèri**) boatyard where gondolas are made

stracaganàse dried chestnuts (the name means "jaw-strainers")

stròpolo bottle top or cork

sùca pumpkin

sùgoli sweet made with American grapes and flour

sùpa soup

tabàro (plural **tabàri**) cloak

tècia pan or frying pan

tegolìne French beans

tetìna cow's udder

tirimesù (or **tiramisù** - the name means "pick-me-up") sweet made with layers of coffee-soaked biscuits, mascarpone cream cheese and eggs; the sweet is then sprinkled with cocoa powder; the coffee and the calories are guaranteed to give anyone a lift...

tochèto (plural **tochèti**) a small piece; diminutive of **tòco**

tòcio sauce; **tociàr** means to dip or dunk bread in sauce

tòco (plural **tòchi**) piece; diminutive **tochèto**

tòla table

torbolìn very young wine that is still cloudy, not clear; *tórbido* is the Italian for "cloudy" (October-November)

tramezzìno (standard Italian: plural **tramezzìni**) sandwich of white bread with crust removed

vàlle (plural **vàlli**) a part of the lagoon marked or fenced off, or bounded by an embankment, used for fish farming

vaporétto (standard Italian: plural **vaporétti**) water bus

vedèlo (plural **vedèli**) calf

viéro (plural **viéri**) a floating, usually circular, container used as a temporary keepnet for fish or shellfish, especially when selecting **moèche**, **spiàntani** and **masanéte**; also used for collecting **schìe**

vìno da meditazióne (standard Italian: plural **vìni da meditazióne**) a complex, often medium-sweet or sweet wine to savour on its own, or perhaps with nuts or biscuits, rather than with a meal

vóngola veràce (standard Italian: plural **vóngole veràci**) edible bivalve, the cross-cut carpet shell (*Tapes decussatus*)

vòvo (plural **vòvi**) egg; half a boiled egg, **mèso vòvo**, is a popular bar snack

zabaiòn (standard Italian **zabaglióne** or **zabaióne**) a custard of egg yolk, sugar, cinnamon and sweet fortified wine

zalèto (plural **zalèti**) typical yellow-coloured biscuit made with cornflour, sugar, eggs and raisins

zalèti

Printed in June 2004, at Grafiche Vianello, Ponzano/Treviso

Baconi

Celestia

ac Do Marie

da Dante

Oliva nera

da Remigio

Ospedale Civile

Bandierette

alla Mascareta

Fondamente Nuove

Boccadoro

da Sergio

alle Testiere

Agriturbagio

alla Frasca

al Ponte